To Sis. Fay,
You have been such a Bo to me the last to years. Continue to be a Virtuous Woman.

Love,
J.

DEAR DAUGHTER

HOW TO CHOOSE YOUR WAY TO A BETTER **LIFE**

TIJUANNA ADETUNJI

The Dear Daughter Series Book One

TOMF Publishing

DEAR DAUGHTER:
HOW TO CHOOSE YOUR WAY TO A BETTER LIFE
Book One
Published by TOMF, Inc
PO Box 242492, Montgomery, AL 36124

© 2008 by Tijuanna Adetunji
International Standard Book Number: 978-0-9819390-0-1
Cover design by John Crenshaw

Printed in the United States of America

ALL RIGHTS RESERVED

No part of this book may be reproduced, stored in a retrieval system, or transmitted in any form by any means—electronic, mechanical, photocopy, recording, or otherwise—without prior written permission of the publisher,

Scripture quotations marked (NLT) are taken from the *Holy Bible*, New Living Translation, copyright © 1996. Used by permission of Tyndale House Publishers, Inc., Wheaton, Illinois 60189.
All rights reserved.

Scripture quotations marked (NIV) are taken from the HOLY BIBLE, NEW INTERNATIONAL VERSION®. NIV®. Copyright© 1973, 1978, 1984 by International Bible Society. Used by permission of Zondervan. All rights reserved.

Library of Congress Control Number: 2008911004

Includes bibliographical references.

Table of Contents

	Dedication	6
	Acknowledgements	7
	Preface	8
1.	Be teachable…	10
2.	Get moral counsel…	16
3.	See the miracle…	22
4.	Be aware of your emotions…	28
5.	Have faith…	34
6.	Don't follow…	40
7.	The choice is…	47
8.	When given the opportunity…	53
	Reflections	60
	A note to Moms…	68
	Endnotes	76

In Memory of
Mrs. Otis Mae Jones and Ms. M.E. Thorn

Dedication

To my very own daughter Ashlen Cuyler and every young woman who is looking for the right answers in this world full of choices.
Be of good courage, and he shall strengthen your heart, all ye that hope in the Lord.
Psalm 31:24

Acknowledgements

To my Father God, thank you for sending your Son. His love is amazing for He is my consolation.

To my husband Pastor Frederick Adetunji, thank you for your continuous love, provision, encouragement, covering and night time prayers.

To my three sons James, Joshua, and Kyle, you guys are the greatest.

To my Parents Annie Reeves and Joe Reeves, thank you for giving me life. Mom, thank you for years of continuous sacrifice. You made everywhere feel like home.

To Pastors Kyle and Kemi Searcy, thank you for demonstrating the power of passion towards Jesus Christ and teaching my hands to war!

To Sheree Finley, thank you for giving your time in the initial editing phase.

To Lynn Vincent thank you for your professional critique and insight. It was priceless.

A special thanks to those who have labored for the sanctity of human life.

Preface

This book began almost three years ago as a letter that I wrote to my then sixteen-year old daughter who thought as though she was, "The Little Engine That Could." That said, "I think I can, I think I can." And I was saying, "No you can't, not yet!

As the conductor of the train I had been down that road before and have several scars to prove it. So, I began to flash the yellow and red lights indicating that there was danger ahead. In my own way I was shouting, "Slow down, watch out, stop, or at the least, wait!"

In her own way she was shouting back, "The road looks clear to me, I got this!"

The road always looks clear when you're looking straight ahead. It's the curves, blind spots, and the trash in the road that gets you.

In the midst of writing this book there were many challenges. There were times when I could not just tell my daughter not to do this or that. I had to help her decipher what the trash in the road was. I had to show her how to see when you're blinded and how to make it around a curve without falling over.

Making decisions down this road called life is not easy. However, it can be less painful especially if you've been informed.

Therefore, this book is an informative way of giving young women a heads up. Within its pages you get an inside look at the choices that I made as a young woman that had an adverse affect on me.

As a guide each chapter bares a sign to instruct you along the way with a time to reflect on what you've read at the end. I hope that you will prayerfully consider the directions given and use them as you travel on your own journey of life.

CHAPTER ONE

BE TEACHABLE AND LEARN FROM OTHERS

"The best learning I had came from teaching."
Corrie Ten Boon

Dear Daughter,

I am writing this letter because I love you and to tell you that I understand this very important phase of your life in becoming a woman. You are at the age of assuming responsibility, which includes making major decisions and choices when I am not right by your side. I hope that my experiences will help you choose a better path on this journey of life. I believe there are three types of paths that you can take. They are:

1. **Easy**—This path is taken by those who have observed the lives of others that have endured hard consequences as a result of their choices. The person that takes this way gains insight from others and uses it in their own decision making.
2. **Hard**—On this road a person chooses not to take road No. 1 and decides to try things out for themselves. However, they later realize their choice was not a good one after all. Fortunately, they learn valuable lessons from their own experience which enables them to make better choices in the future.
3. **Tragic**—This is the worst path of all. The person that travels this

road does not adhere to No. 1 or 2. They never learn, not even from their own mistakes.

My Momma used to tell me, "You can't see for looking." I would say to myself (I did not talk back to my Momma), "What are you talking about?" "That doesn't make any sense."

Amazingly, it makes perfectly good sense to me now. She was implying that I needed to stop looking all over for answers. I should be still, listen to what she was saying, and look at some of the choices that she had made. What I had in front of me (my Mom) could have been the answer. If only I would have taken time to appreciate and learn from her.

In other words, young people have a tendency to think that older people are old fashioned and do not know what they are talking about. Older people may not be as "down" as you are with the latest fashions but they have a wealth of wisdom that you can glean from if you listen.

Solomon, the wisest man that ever lived said, "Nothing under the sun is truly new" (Ecclesiastes 1:9 NLT).

My desire is that you have a fulfilled life. However, just as my Mom was trying to give me advice when I was your age I did not receive it. Unknowingly, I had built up barriers that kept me from listening. Make sure you do not have those same barriers in place. This is what they can look like:

- **Pride**—a high or inordinate opinion of one's own dignity, importance, merit, or superiority, whether as cherished in the mind, or as displayed in bearing, conduct, etc.[1]
- **Presumption**—to take something for granted; suppose.[2]
- **Fantasy**—a supposition based on no solid foundation; visionary idea.[3]

Be Teachable And Learn From Others

Having pride as a barrier will keep you from receiving advice from certain people because of their age, social status, appearance and even race. Presumption makes you unappreciative. What you have never seems to be good enough. This barrier can cause you to always look at your own needs and never consider the needs of others. Fantasy or fantasizing can cause you to remain in a perpetual dream world and never deal with reality.

Some of the most popular programs on television today are the so-called "reality" shows. Do they really depict reality? Some times yes, when it comes to building a house, repairing a broken window or learning how to cook.

Unfortunately, there are others that depict a Mr. and Ms. Right or even worse two men and two women living lifestyles of perpetual romance and freedom. That is not reality and "freedom is not free." Ask our US Military servicemen that have fought in a war zone and they will tell you about the high cost of freedom. In fact, anyone who partakes in a freedom outside of the boundaries of its purpose will have to pay a price.

I paid a painful price because I did not fully understand the responsibility of my freedom of choice. I chose path No.2, and had to learn from my mistakes. Although others in our family had taken the same road, I could not interpret their silent signals of regret.

Therefore, Daughter, I am openly sharing the truth about my journey so that you do not waste years of your life before you get this understanding. It's for you now!

CHAPTER TWO

GET MORAL COUNSEL BEFORE MAKING MAJOR DECISIONS

"Do not open your heart to every man, but discuss your affairs to one who is wise and fears God."

Thomas a Kempis

When I was seven years old my father came to visit me. This was his first visit since he and my mom separated shortly after I was born. He brought me a gift, a little wooden jewelry box that had the words "hope chest" written on it. As I look back now, I realize that those words were prophetic or a forewarning of what was to take place in my life.

As I grew older, and became a young woman just as you are now, I hoped and longed to have a relationship with my father. I longed to see him and spend time with him. It was not because he had been involved in my life. It was because he was my father and there was something on the inside of me that wanted to get to know him.

◊ I KNOW HOW YOU FEEL ◊

I was composed of his DNA. I had his genes. I could not understand why a father would not want his own child. How could he not think of me? How could he not call or write? I certainly thought of him.

I then made a vow to myself, saying, "I am never going to allow my child to go through this abandonment. I am going to grow up, go to college, have a career, get married, have children and live happily ever after.

Since I was hoping and longing for this love, I found myself looking in all the wrong places. In the arms of this boy and that boy; then it grew into the arms of this man and that man. I was not looking for sex. I just wanted their love and affirmation. I did not realize that one did not come without the other.

◊ HOPE DEFERRED ◊

Do not be deceived by these types of sexual relationships. Intimate activity with out a marriage commitment first, is a dead end. At age seventeen, during my senior year in high school I found myself pregnant. Although I was young, unmarried and not doing things the right way, I somehow expected things to turn out right.

In fact, I was in the middle of an unfavorable trend that has swept across this country. The number of pregnancies to unmarried teens has increased dramatically from 13% in 1950 to 79% in 2000.[4]

As an American woman, I had and still have the legal right to do with my body whatsoever I choose. That right includes if I am pregnant I can end the life of my child at anytime during the pregnancy. Therefore, without my mothers' knowledge, even though I was considered a minor in every other instance I was able to abort my unborn child at age seventeen. The laws differ by state. Currently in Alabama there is a 24-hr waiting period.

My reasoning's were, I could not bear the thought of this baby not having his father and I did not want to be another statistic, an unwed African American teen mother. I had know idea that I was adding to the worst statistics ever:

- 35% of abortions in the U.S are performed on African American women although they make up only 13% of the female population.[5]

Get Moral Counsel Before Making Major Decisions

- Abortion is the leading killer among African Americans-not violent crimes, AIDS, stroke, heart attack or cancer.[6]

How did we as Americans get here? To tell you the complete story I would have to go all the way back to the book of *Genesis*, the place where mankind first decided to go his own way in the "Garden of Eden." However, you've heard the cliché, "When you point one finger at someone else there are four more pointing back at you."

Specifically within the African American community there are several real issues that have contributed holistically to the current state of the family. For example; absentee and incarcerated fathers, dependency on the governmental welfare system, single parent households, and cohabitation, which my great-grandmother called "shacking up." That is when two people live together as if they are married but they're not. She also called it playing house like children. Neither person is mature enough to make a real commitment.

When my great-grandmother was a teen and young adult they would rather have a "shotgun marriage" than none at all. That is after realizing the girl was pregnant they would marry and make a commitment to one another before the child was born. This was done not to allow the child to be born illegitimately.

They understood personal responsibility. At some point, we have to hold ourselves accountable for our on actions regardless of influences and circumstances.

You can avoid being irresponsible by not making isolated decisions including those where your peers give you counsel. If you needed help with your algebra homework would you go to the person who's struggling like you are? Or would you go to the person who is making A's. Of course you would go to the person making good grades and know what they are talking about.

Get Moral Counsel Before Making Major Decisions

Daughter, many of life's dilemmas are not as simple as a math problem and going to friends is often quick and convenient. Do not settle for what you want to hear but seek the truth from those who have already lived it.

CHAPTER THREE

SEE THE MIRACLE IN YOUR LIFE AND FIND PURPOSE IN IT

"Impossible situations can become possible miracles."
                                    Robert H. Schuller

My search continued even after the traumatic experience at age seventeen. Determined to reach my life goals, I began to think that maybe I needed self-discipline. I joined the Army Reserves thinking that surely they could do something with someone like me. In the midst of my enlistment, my search and desire for this missing love overruled my desire for discipline. Therefore, I found myself in another relationship.

◊ MERRY-GO-ROUND ◊

Still determined to follow through on my plans, I came back and enrolled into college. Now nineteen years of age and to my surprise, I was pregnant again. I was not surprised because it was not possible for me to get pregnant, I just didn't bargain on it happening to me. I still did not understand that every action brings a reaction in some form.

This time I did not know what I was going to do. I isolated myself as much as possible and did not tell any of my friends or family members that I was pregnant. Unfortunately, I still had the same self-absorbed convictions that lacked insight and direction.

Therefore, I selfishly decided it would be better for this child not to be here either. I contemplated about what to do for weeks. Those weeks turned into months. After I had already decided what I was going to do I had to further convince myself to justify what I was doing. I then made up the following excuses:

"I am not ready for this responsibility."
"I'm not married."
"I'm black."
"I'm not seemingly going anywhere."
"I have nothing to give this baby."

Pride mixed with presumption and fantasy creates a tricky dynamic. In the midst of them I blindly became who I did not want to be. This reminds me of an ancient prophecy in the Old Testament book of Isaiah given to the King of Babylon. His attitude was contrasted with the heart of Lucifer himself, the father of pride. It states:

"For you have said to yourself, I will ascend to heaven and set my throne above God's stars.

> I will preside on the mountain of the gods far away in the north.
> I will climb to the highest heavens and be like the Most High.

Instead you will be brought down to the place of the dead, down to its lowest depths" (Isaiah 14:13-15 NLT).

The major attribute of pride is that it will always exalt itself above everything else and will not allow any considerations for logical reasoning. Watch out for it. No one is exempt.

◊ DESTINED TO BE HERE ◊

With my mind made up. I found a clinic that did late term abortions about 100 miles away and drove myself there. Before finally going in, I waited around still contemplating about what to do. They called me to a room in the back. A woman examined my stomach and said, "Go home you are about to have a baby in a few weeks." After that, I finally accepted the fact that I was really going to have a baby unmarried at nineteen.

Daughter, you are truly a miracle. I wish that I could say that it was my love that saved you. However, I cannot take any of the credit. People always say to me how beautiful you are and how much we look a like. Again, I cannot take any of the credit. It was God that saved you and gave you to me and I'm so glad he did.

I urge you not to take your life for granted. Since January 22, 1973 the date that the Supreme Court concluded in the case of *Roe v. Wade* which gave women the legal right to end their pregnancies.[7] Since then there have been approximately 48,589,993 abortions in America.[8] Out of those, 14 million have been African American.[9] You are truly a *Survivor,*[10] those that made it out alive after the legalization of abortion in America.

Perhaps you were born for "such a time as this" (Esther 4:14NLT) like a young woman named Hadassah, also known as Esther. An entire book of the Bible was written about her. In the book it describes how Esther interceded or acted on the behalf of those in trouble by placing her own life on the line. In the end she was responsible for saving her entire race from extermination. Were you saved for a time like this? What will you be known for? How will you help your generation? Think about it.

CHAPTER FOUR

BEWARE OF YOUR EMOTIONS THEY CAN CAUSE YOUR DECISIONS TO BE DEVASTATING

"The right to life does not depend, and must not be declared to be contingent, on the pleasure of anyone else, not even a parent or a sovereign."
Mother Teresa

As beautiful as you were when you were born and as much as I loved you, I wish that I could say that my search for love came to an end. In fact, I made several other attempts to find it. Another man came across my path.

He seemed to be perfect, in control and with everything in place. I soon found out he was separated from his wife. That means he was still married. If you are ever approached by a married man send him home and run for your life.

◊ BLINDED EYES ◊

There I was again twenty-five years old asking myself the same questions as I did when I was seventeen. I was pregnant again in the worst relationship ever. Silly me, there I was again back in the valley of decision uninformed and without direction. I selfishly aborted again this being the second time. After the procedure, I was in excruciating pain.

I ached physically and emotionally. Emotionally because I was just as empty as I was before, but worse. I had put all I had into this man only to find out that I was still looking for true love in the wrong place. I ached physically because the procedure was done improperly (not that an abortion is ever proper). I had to go back to that dreadful abortion clinic. A part of the child was left inside of me. They call it retained tissue. It is not tissue. It is a human being. Abortion is a murderous procedure that many women choose for numerous reasons.

Some are even persuaded because of incest at such a young age. Even as I am telling you this story, I can still hear the sound of the vacuum. I deeply regret my choices of having an abortion. I think about the children that could have been. For a long period of time I ignored the fact that it even happened. You should know that it has been my acknowledging the truth of my terrible choice and not suppression of it that has enabled me to speak openly.

I plead to you daughters, never do this. Wait until you are ready to assume full responsibility of having a child before you engage in what it takes to get one. However, there is help for those of you that are in a crisis, including victims of incest (rape by relative). I will list them at the end of this letter.

By now I was very confused because I had done all that I knew to find this love. Even before that last episode, two years earlier I did some research and found my Dad. I traveled from Montgomery, Alabama to Akron, Ohio all on a whim hoping to find him. I only had an old address.

◊ ALL OUT SEARCH ◊

When I arrived in Ohio, I went from house to house, street to street looking for my Dad. After hours of searching, I finally found him. I had grown to look more like him than my mother. I have his facial profile, skin complexion, hair, his stature, everything. The only difference is that I'm a woman.

Our time together was brief, but it was a good reunion. I kept in contact with him and he even moved to Alabama and lived with me for a while. Even though I was an adult, the time with my Dad was well spent and I am very grateful for that time. However, I noticed something about myself. I still felt very empty. I thought that hugs, affirmations, and talks with my Dad would somehow make me feel better, but I was still empty. There was something still missing.

◊ SEEK AND YOU SHALL FIND ◊

I began to contemplate and ask myself some questions. What is wrong with me? What is wrong with my heart and why can't I find fulfillment? Why are my plans failing? Why am I not being satisfied? As soon as I began to ask those questions I began to get answers. The answers did not come from my own intellect. I obviously did not know. For years I had been going around the same circle of not adhering to any signs not even my own emotions.

Amazingly, a woman by the name of Mrs. Emma Williams gave my friend a cassette tape of a pastor teaching from the Holy Bible.

She brought it to me and said, "You have got to listen to this now."

He was talking about running away from fornication, sex and fondling outside of marriage. He explained how it feels good for the moment but the result of it is destruction, heartache and pain and that the wages of sin is death (Romans 6:23). He explained that sin is what separates man from God and the end result of it is destruction.

In all my years of going in and out of church as a young person, I had never heard those words before. The message was as if he was speaking directly to me and for the first time I began to listen and adhere to the signs.

Chapter Five

HAVE FAITH
ITS A GOOD THING

"Faith never knows where it is being led, but it loves and knows the One who is leading."
                                             Oswald Chambers

After I heard that practical message based on Biblical truths I begin to think about my life. In fact, it all flashed right before my eyes. The hard times I witnessed my mother experience. The times when I was partying at nightclubs and there was gunfire; the time when I fell asleep at the wheel and my car drifted in front of an eighteen-wheeler; the time when I was choked unconsciously by a jealous boyfriend; the deaths of my unborn children at the abortion clinics and so much more.

I could sense that there had been mercy on my life. I then asked a question, "What can I do to recompense for my many wrong choices?"

A voice responded by saying, "Nothing, but now you can present your body to me as a living sacrifice and give me praise" (Romans 12:1KJV).

At the time I did not understand the meaning of that verse. But I responded by saying, "Yes, I will do it with your help."

When I said yes, the love that I had been looking for since my father gave me that hope chest began to overtake me. It was and still is so awesome that at times I shout in a loud voice to him with adoration and praise. It's the same way you do for your favorite team at a basketball or football game. Along with it came joy, peace, inner healing, restoration of things lost and even the hope that had been deferred. Until then that was the only love that was able to console my pain. Even now when I think I am filled to capacity, he shows me another side of himself. My own words cannot adequately describe who he is.

In the book of the Bible called Song of Solomon or Song of Songs, it talks about a young woman who found this same love that I'm telling you about. He loved her and desired for her to grow up and become mature. To cultivate her growth he pulled away and went to higher heights so that she would follow him.

Unfortunately, when he called her to come, she did what we all sometimes do; take our time and make excuses. He left immediately. When she got up to look for him, he was gone. Since she had tasted and experienced his love, she did not want to live without it. She then began to search for him. She even searched during the night.

During that time, it was not customary for women to be out during the night alone. However, in her desperation and pain of being separated from the one she loved, she risked being talked about.

She even told the watchmen, "If you see him please tell him how much I miss him."

You'll recognize him when you see him. He looks like none other. He looks like this:

"My lover is dark and dazzling,
better than ten thousand others!
His head is the finest gold,
And his hair is wavy and black.
His eyes are like doves
beside brooks of water;
they are set like jewels.
His cheeks are like sweetly scented
beds of spices.
His lips are like perfumed lilies.
His breath is like myrrh.
His arms are like round bars of gold,
set with chrysolite.
His body is like bright ivory,

aglow with sapphires.
His legs are like pillars of marble
set in sockets of the finest gold,
strong as the cedars of Lebanon.
None can rival him.
His mouth is altogether sweet;
he is lovely in every way.
Such women of Jerusalem,
is my lover, my friend."
Song of Songs 5:10-16 NLT

After the watchmen heard the description of the one she loved, they asked her a question, "Who is this and which way did he go? We want to help you find him."

In that same book of the Bible over in chapter eight verse seven it says:

"Many waters cannot quench love, neither can floods drown it: if a man would give all the substance of his house for love, it would utterly be contemned." (NLT)

In other words, the fire of pure love cannot easily be quenched and building one's love and life on material things is in vain.

CHAPTER SIX

DON'T FOLLOW THE CROWD—LEAD THEM

"A leader takes people where they want to go. A great leader takes people where they don't necessarily want to go, but ought to be".
                              Rosalyn Carter

To paint an even better picture, I must tell you about two other women who also had extraordinary encounters with this kind of love. The first is a Samaritan woman. Her story is found in the New Testament book of the Bible in the fourth chapter of the gospel of John.

This story takes place at a rest stop where people came to draw water from a well. The Samaritan woman came to the well as she normally did everyday. There was a man there that she had never seen before. He was not a local; he was different.

◊ THIRST QUENCHED ◊

As she was about to draw her water, this man said to her, "Will you give me a drink?"

Then she went on to explain to him that she was of one race and he was of another and who was he to ask her for a drink. She deemed herself superior to him implying that she wasn't even supposed to be talking to him.

He was aware of the local customs. However, he was not intimidated.

He told her if she knew what God was trying to give her she would be asking him to give her a drink. Since the water he had was living water. He then answered her and said, "If you really knew who I was you would ask me to give you a drink of what I have. The water I have is living and if you drink of me you will never thirst again."

She then said, "Give me some of the water that you are referring to so that I may never thirst again."

Guess what he said? "Before I do that, go call your husband, and tell him to come here."

Then she said, "I do not have a husband."

Then he said, "You got that right. You have had five husbands and the one you are with now is not yours either."

He did not embarrass her but he confronted the truth. She said, "You must be a prophet because what you just said about me is true."

She had heard about his teaching and other miracles but because of the local traditions she continued to follow the crowd. Now she knew it for herself. He further explained that if she wanted him and his living water, she must worship him in spirit and in truth. She must have accepted his invitation because she threw down her water pot and ran into the city shouting to everyone, "LOOK! COME SEE THIS MAN THAT TOLD ME EVERYTHING THAT I EVER DID!"

The Samaritan woman found the one person that knew all about her and still invited her to come and partake of his love.

◊ NO HOLDING BACK ◊

The second woman is the boldest of them all. This story is found in the seventh chapter of the gospel of Luke. A religious leader of the city wanted to personally meet this man. He invited him to his house for dinner in order to check him out.

As a result, he accepted the invitation. In the midst of dinner, an uninvited woman forced her way into the dining room. She went and stood behind the man and wepted. She began to wash his feet with her tears. She dried his feet with her hair and kissed them with her lips. She then broke the seal off of her greatest possession; an alabaster box filled with expensive perfume, and anointed his feet.

Simon, the religious leader, when he saw this, he said inwardly, "I knew that he was not a prophet. If he was he would know what kind of woman was touching him."

She was a sinner, one who has committed many wrongs. This man who knows all things knew what Simon was thinking so he called him out by name and said, "Simon, let me tell you a story."

Did I mention he is the master of all storytelling? He said, "There was a man that loaned two people money. He gave 500 hundred pieces of silver to one and 50 pieces to the other. Neither of them could repay him, so he kindly forgave them both and canceled their debts. Who do you think loved him the most after that?"

Simon said, "The one who he forgave the most." "Then he said, look at this woman kneeling here." When I came into your home you did not offer me water to wash the dust from my feet, but she washed them with her tears and wiped them with her hair."

He went on to say, "You did not greet me with a kiss, but from the time I got here, she has not stopped kissing my feet. You did not give me any olive oil to anoint my head, but she has anointed my feet with rare perfume."

◊ GOING FORTH ◊

He then told her that her sins were forgiven, it was faith that saved her and to go in peace. She knew that he was the only one capable of doing this. Having come to the end of herself, she no longer cared about the opinions of others. She now had forgiveness, joy, peace and most of all his love.

Who is this man that quenches the thirst of those who are thirsty and fills the souls of those who are hungry? His name is JESUS! Hallelujah! He is altogether lovely! In the Matthew 11:28-30 he says:

"Come to me, all of you who are weary and carry heavy burdens, and I will give you rest. Take my yoke upon you. Let me teach you, because I am humble and gentle at heart, and you will find rest for your souls. For my yoke is easy to bear, and the burden I give you is light." (NLT)

CHAPTER SEVEN

THE CHOICE IS YOURS

"It's choice —not chance — that controls your destiny."

Zig Ziglar

Daughter, you were five years old when I first heard the voice of God. Since then I have tried to teach you and all your friends who would listen what I've learned. By God's grace, for the rest of my days I will do my best to continue to share with all of you and be an example.

However, it is now your turn to seek this love out for yourself. One thing I know for certain is that the more you seek him, the more you will find him.

Just as my earthly father gave me that hope chest as a gift when I was seven years old, your heavenly Father is offering you a much better gift today. It will never tarnish or fade away. That gift is eternal life.

Your sins may not be like mine or the other women mentioned in this letter but all it takes is one offense to be found guilty. Nevertheless, God loves you so much that he sent his only begotten Son and if you believe in him you will not perish but have everlasting life (John 3:16NLT).

The way that you accept him is through your own freewill by doing the following:

1. **Acknowledge that you are a sinner.** For everyone has sinned; we all fall short of God's glorious standard (Romans 3:23, NLT).

But the scriptures declare that we are all prisoners of sin, so we receive God's promise of freedom only by believing in Jesus Christ (Gal.3:23).

2. Believe in your heart that God raised him from the dead.

...I am the resurrection and the life. Anyone who believes in me will live, even after dying (John 11:25NLT).

For it is by believing in your heart that you are made right with God... (Ro.10:10a NLT).

3. Confess with your mouth that Jesus is Lord.

If you confess with your mouth that Jesus is Lord and believe in your heart that God raised him from the dead you will be saved (Ro.10:9NLT).

Everyone who acknowledges me publicly here on earth, I will also acknowledge before my Father in heaven (Matt.10:32 NLT).

Finally, no one knows their day or hour of death. As a former life insurance agent I have had many people call me for an insurance policy after they or a family member have been diagnosed with a terminal illness or are on their death bed. It is unwise to wait until you're dying to get your final expenses in order.

It is also unwise to think that there will be time to prepare for eternity. Preparation must be made in advance. As a young person you are prone to think that you have so much time, at least 70 years. That is not necessarily true. In some instances a teen or young adult are more liable to die before an older person. For instance, while driving, 15 to 19-year-olds have not only one of the highest death rates, but their passengers riding with them many of whom are also teenagers.[11]

In 2006, there were reportedly 5,159 teens ages 13-19 that died from a car accident, compared to 4,636 people that were over the age of 70 that also died from a car accident.[12] Death has no preference of age. However, we all must be ready. The Bible clearly states:

"And it is appointed unto men once to die, but after this the judgment."(Heb.9:27a)

"For we must all stand before Christ to be judged. We will each receive whatever we deserve for the good or evil we have done in this earthly body."(2Cor. 5:10 NLT)

I think about all of the bright and shiny things that you like. However, when I think about eternity nothing can compare. I too do not know my hour of death. Nevertheless, I am ready and prepared. I have even asked my self a series of questions concerning you.

- What would I want to leave you with the most?
- Of the things left, what would make the most difference in your life?
- What could help you make it through any situation or circumstance?

The answer to each question is resoundingly that I told you about the man named Jesus Christ and that you got to know Him for yourself. This is my hope and gift of LIFE to you.

Love Mom

CHAPTER EIGHT

When Given The Opportunity To Speak—Say The Right Thing

"Darkness cannot drive out darkness; only light can do that. Hate cannot drive out hate; only love can do that."

Martin Luther King Jr.

P.S Although I've placed my closing remarks at the end of this letter, wisdom tells me that the story should not end there. You probably have something to say too. Perhaps it's something that you've been holding inside. As your Mother, even in my trying to do or say the right thing, it can sometimes come out wrong. Therefore, I would like to give you an opportunity to say what's on your heart back to me in writing. From experience I've learned that unforgiveness is the lock that holds us hostage but forgiveness is the key that sets us free. As you write me back, I am asking you to forgive me for anything I've done or did not do that caused you to take offense or stumble.

Some of your friends that are reading this letter may no longer have their Mom. Some even may not even know who she is. Nevertheless, all of you have something to say. We all have different backgrounds with different ways we grew up. However, we all have one common thread. We all have something to be thankful for.

After you take time to write out your thoughts and lay aside the unforgiveness, I want you to write out the things that you are thankful for concerning your Mom.

The common thread that we can all thank our Mothers for is that through God she gave us LIFE. Isn't that wonderful! Also, since you are reading this letter, it means that you are breathing and are still alive. Therefore, you have purpose and a chance to place those things that have been holding you back aside.

On the following pages start out with giving thanks, then forgive others, and most importantly forgive yourself. In the space provided and in your own personal journal I also encourage you to reflect on what you learned in each chapter and what it means to you.

Dear Mom,

Thank you for...

When Given The Opportunity To Speak-Say The Right Thing

I forgive you for...

I forgive others in my life for…

When Given The Opportunity To Speak-Say The Right Thing

I also forgive myself for...

Reflections

a fixing of thoughts on something; careful consideration.

Chapter 1

1. What does it mean to teachable?

2. Of the three types of paths listed: easy, hard, and tragic describe which one you are on and why.

3. What are the three barriers that can keep you from learning and have you allowed any of these barriers in your life?

Chapter 2

1. The title of this chapter is *Get Moral Counsel Before Making Major Decisions*. What does the word moral mean?

2. What does it mean to take personal responsibility?

3. List some ways that you can began to become more responsible.

Chapter 3

1. Are you or someone you know currently in what seems to be an impossible situation? If so contact the organizations in the back of the book listed under the *Need Help Now* section for further instructions and options.

2. In this chapter several excuses were made that were later regretted. Do you have any excuses? If so list them and tell how they may lead to something you're not proud of later.

3. What type of impact will you have on your generation?

Chapter 4

1. Your emotions are often indicators of what's going on inside. What are your emotions telling you?

2. This chapter illustrates how the same mistake can be made over again. How can you live differently to avoid this?

3. How should you respond when you hear the truth about what you're doing?

Chapter 5

1. The word faith is synonymous with belief, trust, and reliance. What does having faith mean to you?

2. Up until now what have you been putting your faith in?

3. Which one is more important, having faith, or what you have your faith in?

Reflections

Chapter 6

1. When the woman at the well acknowledged the truth about her past she was able to go and freely tell others. What are some things about your past that you need to acknowledge?

2. The second woman demonstrated her gratitude even at the risk of being misunderstood. Are you willing to express your gratefulness? If so how will you do it?

3. Sin is a deed of disobedience to a divine law that will be judged. It was faith that saved the second woman. Are you willing to exercise faith so that your judgment want be detrimental?

Chapter 7

1. Fill in the blank from the quote from the beginning of the chapter: "It's choice _____ _____ that controls your destiny." What does that mean?

2. We can speculate how long we will live but we do not know. However, we should be prepared for when that time comes. Have you had a chance to prepare?

3. Which is more valuable, possessions (jewelry, cars, houses) or eternal things like faith? Explain why.

Reflections

Chapter 8

1. Explain: Unforgiveness is the lock that holds us hostage but forgiveness is the key that sets us free.

2. How does it feel to forgive others and yourself?

3. What was the thing you were most thankful for concerning your Mom? Were there other things that you didn't list?

A Note to Present & Future Moms

"Above all, we (as parents) must make sure that the open book of our lives–our example–demonstrates the reality of our instruction, for in watching us they will learn the most".

Kent Hughes

Dear Moms,

Also as a former medic in the Army Reserves, during combat training we were taught how to treat our own wounds first so that we could help others on the field. By doing this, we could live in order to save someone else to fight again and ultimately win the war.

A Note To Present & Future Moms

Unfortunately, as mothers we try to be superwomen. We take on fulfilling the needs of everyone else while ignoring our own needs. We go and go, saying we will get to taking care of ourselves one day and that day never comes. Before we realize it, years have gone by and we never took time to deal with past hurts, unforgiveness, shattered dreams and even traumas from as far back as our childhood.

Unknowingly these things can shape us and cause us to feel depressed, condemned, inadequate and some times even angry. We then unknowingly pass these characteristic traits on to our children.

Believe me I know, bringing up children is not an easy task. However, if we are going to lead by example we must become intentional by taking off the mask. No longer should we hide behind the symptoms of our past. Join me in my forthcoming study-guide, *Moms Unmasked*, where we encourage one another and confront traumatic events from our past to enable us to become better women, mothers, and wives.

By being transparent we will defy the norm and allow the love and strength of the Almighty God to overtake and reshape us into the women that He has ordained us to be. And as we are consumed and changed so shall this generation be. Consume us Lord!

Next in the Dear Daughter Series & More

Book Two
Dear Daughter: How to Be Set Apart In an Everything Goes World
Dare to value yourself! As you do you'll be priceless.

Dear Daughter: Leader Training Manual
An aid to facilitate small group sessions with the Dear Daughter Series of books for young women.

Moms Unmasked
A revelatory workbook style study-guide that helps to restore women after an abortion and surrounding events.

More Instructions & Tools

This list provided in this Dear Daughter Series of Books and beforeyouchoose.org, is provided for information only. Referral to these sites/publications and their advertisements does not imply the endorsement of The Opportunity Makers Foundation Inc., and or its programs or activities. This list is not comprehensive. Please note that sites and URLs are subject to change without warning.

Need Help Now
1-800-395-HELP (4351) or online
www.optionline.org
Rape, Abuse & Incest Nat'l Network 1-800-656-Hope
Informative Websites
www.beforeyouchoose.org
www.blackgenocide.org
www.urbancure.org
www.protectingblacklife.org
www.lifeissues.org
Books & Publications
Why Pro-Life? Randy Alcorn, Eternal Perspective Ministries, www.epm.org
Did You Know?, Just for Girls, Just for Guys
www.humanlifealliance.org
DVD- Truth Unmasked – Lifeissues.org

Contact TOMF for information on discounts available for quantities of this book.

TOMF
P.O. Box 242492
Montgomery, AL 36124
Phone: 334-613-3363 ext. 203
email: tomf@beforeyouchoose.org

Dear Daughter:
How to Choose Your Way To A Better Life
ISBN 978-0-9819390-0-1

About the Author

Tijuanna Adetunji is an inspirational speaker and writer using her past experience and ongoing interaction with young women to encourage them to embrace purity and value life through the love of God.

Tijuanna has served her community as a volunteer pregnancy resource center counselor, benevolence program developer, and food bank distributor to families in need and has traveled to Ghana West Africa to support efforts to build an orphanage.

She and her husband Fred have four children and live in Montgomery, AL. They have been active in their church Fresh Anointing House of Worship for over fourteen years where Fred is the Pastoral Care Pastor and she is a Pastoral Care Minister and has served as a Deaconess and Executive Assistant to the Senior Pastor. However, Tijuanna's favorite area of service is the Inner Healing and Deliverance Ministry where many people find freedom from their past of guilt, shame, addictions, and emotional distress.

She and her husband are also the founders of The Opportunity Makers Foundation Inc., and **beforeyouchoose.org** an interactive web log that encourages women that are in the valley of decision to make an informed choice.

Endnotes

Chapter 1

1,2,3 (pg.13) - Dictionary.com Unabridged (v1.1) Based on the Random House Unabridged Dictionary, © Random House, Inc. 2006

Chapter 2

4 – (pg.18) The Guttmacher Report on Public Policy by Heather Boonstra
http:// www. Guttmacher .org

5 – (pg. 19)Morbidity and Mortality Weekly Report Surveillance Summaries November 23, 2007/Vol.56/No.ss-9 Page 7 www.cdc.gov

6 – (pg.20) United States Census Bureau

Chapter 3

7 – (Pg.27) The Oyez Project, Roe v. Wade, 410 U.S 113 (1973), available at: http://www.oyez.org/cases/1970=1979/1971/1971/ 70 18/

8 – (Pg. 27)National Right To Life – Abortion Facts http://www.nrlc.org
CDC MMWR Surveillance Summary Nov.24, 2006/55 (ss11); 1-32

9 – (pg.27) CDC-Morbidity and Mortality Weekly Report, November 24, 2006 Vol.55/SS-11

10 –(pg.27) Survivors, A Christian Pro-Life Activism Organization http://www.srvivors.la/

Chapter 7

11- (pg.51)National Highway Traffic Safety Administration
http://ww.nhsta.dot.gov/people/outreach/safesobr/18qp2/buak eys.htm

12- (pg.52) Insurance Institute for Highway Safety
www.ihs.org Fatality Facts 2007 (Teenagers) Fatality Facts 2007 (Older People)